Facilitator's Guide

for use with

Mystie's Activities for Bereaved Teens

and

Diary of a Mystical Dragonfly

KIDS' GRIEF RELIEF

Hi, I'm Mystie.
What's
Dragon - You - Down ?

www.KidsGriefRelief.org

A 501(c)(3) NonProfit

Grief Support to Empower Bereaved Children

ISBN: 978-0-9856334-1-7

(softcover book)

Congratulations on deciding to facilitate a student bereavement group!

Your great contribution is giving your students the opportunity to process their grief over the death of a loved one, while empowering them with life affirming skills. This program is not a substitute for professional counseling. It is a program to support students to move through their grief themselves as you create a safe and loving environment.

This course takes into consideration the unique characteristics of Teens. Most activities revolve around the student's willingness to share, as self - expression plays a vital role during this period of a child's life. Thus, the created "tone" of the setting is crucial. Teens who feel safe and secure will be more willing to share their grief experience. Those who feel that they are being heard are more likely to listen to others.

Validation of their challenging experience, no matter how extreme, is crucial. It creates a foundation of unconditional love and acceptance, which is the atmosphere for the success of this course. The validating conversation helps your students understand that their reactions to the death are normal. It helps them see that no matter how "dire" the situation may look, they have the ability to not only move through their grief, but be stronger for their experience. As you practice empathy instead of sympathy, you place yourself in a position to support your children's journey through grief.

Grief is not an experience students "get over". It's an experience they move through. Ultimately, the death of a loved one becomes integrated into their lives. They can then use this experience to help them gain an awareness of their inner power to move through any of life's challenges.

Our deepest intention is that this course supports each student with the knowledge of the power of Changeless Love within them. Change is inevitable, as realized with the death of a loved one. Yet Love remains forever. It's ongoing expression creates a fulfilling life, moment by moment.

Blessings,
Kids' Grief Relief

Program Guidelines

- This is an *Activity-Based* Teen program which consists of this Facilitator's Guide, and a Student's Booklet of 29 Activities (i.e. ***Mystie's Activities***) which students use to construct their own Activity Book.

- This a a Six-Session Program; ideally one Session per week (we recommend no more than two Sessions per week). The Six Sessions are titled:

  - **What is Grief ?**
  - **All About Me**
  - **All About My Loved One**
  - **Self Reflections on Life and Death**
  - **Change Your Thoughts - Change Your Experience**
  - **Release and Celebrate !**

- The Program is written for groups, and works best when students can interact with each other. It can easily and effectively be used for one child, by selecting activities that do not involve other's participation. We recommend that no more than six students be in a group.

- Each Session contains multiple activities about the specified theme. There are enough activities to last between 45 minutes and one hour per session. The number of activities accomplished is a function of the number of students, the allotted time, the amount of discussion, and the choice to either do the activities verbally or in written form.

- It is recommended that the students receive a folder to store their *Mystie's Activities* book/ pages, and personal photos of their loved one.

- For each Session, the facilitator directs the students to the chosen Activities. Some Activites are only generated by the facilitator, so there is no cooresponding numbered activity in the booklet.

Program Guidelines

- *Mystie's Activities* are referenced by activity number (e.g. Activity 8). The Activity number is located at the lower corner of each page (e.g. Activity 9B). Remember some student's Activites are only presented in this document (e.g.Activity 1).

- If it's not possible to get all the written activities completed in one session, activities can be done orally, focusing on the goal of the session. For example, in Activity 14 (*Remembering*), if there isn't enough time for students to write their list, they can orally share their favorite mementos and tell the class where they keep them.

- Collect the folders at the end of each session. The culmination of all the activity sheets becomes each student's personal keepsake awarded at the end of the program. It is a written record of their participation and achievement.

- For each activity, read over the complete procedure before you present it. You know your students best. You may want to skip some steps or add something of your own. Skip any activity that does not fit your student's needs.

- When directed to "read pg.....", either select students to do the reading, or the facilitator can read aloud, as students follow. Note the terms "special person" and "loved one" are used interchangeably in reference to the person for whom the student is grieving.

- Encourage students to bring to class pictures and memorabilia of their loved ones. Always allow time for students to share these items.

- The provided Mystie Mobile is a kinestetic opportunity for students to bend the wings to show how they feel.

- If you have any questions regarding this program, please email us at inquiry@kidsgriefrelief.org

Reguired Facilitator Materials

(Provided Items in Blue)

For All Six Sessions:

Markers/crayons/pens/pencils

Mystie's Activities for Bereaved Teens
Facilitator's Guide
Mystie Mobile
Folder for each student

Additional Needed Materials:

Session#1
Two pieces of large poster board

Session#2
Two blank 8.5x11 papers per student

Session#3
Game Markers and One Die
Candy for prizes
One Blank 8.5x11 paper per student

Session#4
Diary of a Mystical Dragonfly

Session#5
Waste Basket

Scrap paper

Hand mirror

Session#6
**Battery operated tea-lights
for each student**
Food & Drinks for students

*Optional: Graduation Gift
for each student ** *

Kids' Grief Relief sells special **Mystie gifts for children who have completed the course.
Go to www.kidsgriefrelief.org/Products.html
to choose and order the most appropriate items for each student.*

CLASS
SYLLABUS

Class Syllabus

Session #1
<u>What Is Grief?</u>

1. Let's Get Acquainted

2. Confidentiality

3. What Is Grief ?

4. Defining My Grief

5. Everyone Grieves Differently

6. I Am Compassionate

Session #2
<u>All About Me</u>

7. How am I feeling today ?

8. My Timeline

9. My Story

10. Inside / Outside

11. Validating My Greatest Challenge

Session #3
<u>All About My Loved One</u>

12. How Am I Doing ?

13. Roll-A-Memory Game

14. Remembering

15. Reflections

16. My Future

Class Syllabus

Session #4
Self Reflections on Life and Death

17. Am I Feeling Different ?

18. . Reading / Discussing
    Diary of a Mystical Dragonfly

19. What I Can / Cannot
    Control / Change

Session #5
Change Your Thoughts
Change Your Experience

20. Checking In

21. What You Think Matters

22. Affirmations

23. Frame Yourself !

Session #6
Release & Celebrate !

24. Last Look at Posters

25. Letters of Love

26. Honoring Our Loved Ones

27. Forever Calendar

28. Celebrate !

28. ...and now...

Session 1
What is Grief ?

Objectives

- Students become familiar with other students who are grieving.

- Students gain an understanding of Grief.

- Students become comfortable with the natural reactions to a death of someone close to them.

- Students recognize their own personal support system.

- Students learn to practice Compassion for other students who are also grieving.

Materials Needed:
Two pieces of large posterboard

Session 1
<u>What is Grief?</u>
Activities 1-6

<u>Mystie's Activities</u>

1A-B. Let's Get Acquainted

2. Confidentiality

3. What is Grief?

4. Defining My Grief

5A-B. Everyone Grieves Differently

6. I Am Compassionate

Before handing out *Mystie's Activities* :

–Discuss why students are participating in a grief group.

–Discuss the importance of coming to each session.

–Discuss the level of participation: it's their own choice and it's okay not to share.

–Discuss using common courtesies, such as being quiet when someone is speaking, and showing respect to other members.

Activity 1 A-B
Let's Get Aquainted

Grief Support
Group

Poster #1

MY FAMILY MEMBERS

Circle the ones you live with

My lost loved one: _____

Activity 2

Procedure:

- Place a blank piece of poster board where each student can see it. In the middle, write the words "Grief Support Group". Tell students the time and place for the group to meet each week.

- One at a time, ask each student to speak their name and the name of the loved one who has died. Then have them write their name on the poster board, and underneath writes down the name and relationship to the person who died.
  For example, "Jessica Hill" my **grandmother.**

- When completed, direct students to create a solid lined border around the edges of the posterboard, using a colored marker. Tell them that the solid border signifies "what goes on in this group, stays inside the group". Each student creates some part of the border, and the line around should be solid.

- Ask one student to read all the names and relationships on the poster. Tell students they will add drawings and words to this posterboard as the weeks go on.

- Ask students to fill out Activity 1B by listing family members, including Aunts/Uncles, Grandparents, and Pets.

Activity 2
Confidentiality

What goes on in my Grief Support Group, stays in my Grief Support Group.

signed_____

date_____

Who is in my Grief Support Group?

©2016 Kids' Grief Relief
A-2

Procedure:

- Show each student a copy of _Mystie's Activities for Middle School Students._ _Place the bendable Mystie Mobile on the table._

- Tell them to look at the cover as you say: "_Mystie, the mystical dragonfly, is the spokesperson about grief for this program. The dragonfly, in almost every part of the world symbolizes change. Such change brings an understanding of the deeper meaning of life. Dragonflies normally live most of their lives as nymphs. They fly for only a fraction of their lives and usually not more than a few months. Thus, the dragonfly symbolizes and exemplifies the idea of living life to the fullest, moment by moment, even as things change._"

- Direct them to Activity 2, where students sign their name and date to the promise to keep things confidential in the group.

- Next, direct them to write down the names of everyone else in their group. (They can use the poster to copy everyone's name).

Activity 3
What is Grief ?

GRIEF

Poster #2

Procedure:

- Tape a blank piece of poster board on wall. Ask one student to write the word "**GRIEF**" (all in caps) on top of the paper.

- Say: "*Let's make a list of all the feelings and thoughts we are experiencing since the death of our loved one.*"

- Either facilitator or students create list. Here are some suggestions:

very sad	lonely	shocked	unable to focus
upset	can't eat	mad	can't sleep
confused	guilty	sick	overeating
empty	depressed	angry	headaches
bored	glad	in denial	stomach pain
worried	afraid	giving up	uncomfortable
hopeless	bored	scared	keeping to myself

- *NOTE: The two poster boards from this first session are part of the physical environment that should be present for every session.*

Activity 4
Defining My Grief

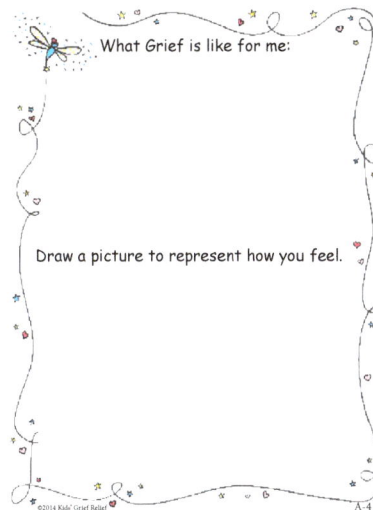

What Grief is like for me:

Draw a picture to represent how you feel.

©2014 Kids' Grief Relief   A-4

Procedure:

- Direct students to Activity 4 in *Mystie's Activities*.

- Tell students to write down the grief phrases that pertain to them (from chart), using specific colors to represent what they feel. For example, a student may choose to use a red marker to write down the word anger, or use a blue marker to write the words very sad.

- Next direct students to draw a picture of how they feel in the bottom box. The drawing can be abstract or not.

- Ask students to share what they have written and explain their drawing to the rest of the group.

Activity 5A
Everyone Grieves Differently

> THERE IS NO "RIGHT WAY" TO GRIEVE.
>
> YOU ARE GRIEVING THE WAY YOU NEED TO.
>
> Other People who are grieving over the death of my loved one:
>
> _____
> _____
> _____
>
> People who are supporting me:
>
> _____
> _____
> _____
> _____

Procedure:

- Direct students to Activity 5, and ask one student to read the top.

- **Tell students the only "wrong" way to grieve is to hurt themselves or others.**

- Students write the names of at least 3 other people who have been affected by the death of their loved one.

- Ask students to tell briefly, how each one of the three is expressing his/her grief.

Activity 5B
Everyone Grieves Differently

THERE IS NO "RIGHT WAY"
TO GRIEVE.

YOU ARE GRIEVING THE
WAY YOU NEED TO.

Other People who are grieving
over the death of my loved one:

_____
_____
_____

People who are supporting me:

_____
_____
_____

©2014 Kids' Grief Relief   A-5

Procedure:

- On the bottom of Activity 5, students write the names of the people who are helping them with their grief. Ask students to share their list with the group.

- DISCUSSION: Ask students how their friends, neighbors, teachers, etc., are treating them since the death of their loved one. Emphasize that it's challenging to know exactly what to say to someone when they're grieving.

Activity 6
I Am Compassionate

What can you say to someone who has lost a loved one? You can speak **Words of Compassion**

"Your _____ loved you a lot. I know you're going to miss her. I bet you have lots of great memories about her."

"I'm sorry to hear about the death of _____. You must miss him very much."

"I know you feel really sad about _____ dying. It's okay to feel sad and upset about it."

"I'm sorry to hear abou the death of your _____. I guess this is a hard time for you."

"I feel sad to hear about the death of your _____. I'm here if you need someone to talk to."

©2014 Kids' Grief Relief

A-6

Procedure:

- Ask a student to read the top of Activity 6.

- Ask students to define Compassion.

- Lead students to the understanding that compassion comes from their heart. It's a warm feeling of understanding that someone is hurting. We practice compassion when we take the time to listen to someone tell about their hurt.

- Ask different students to read the statements listed on the page.

- Start with any student, and ask them to speak one of the sayings to the person on his/her right. Do this so each student gets a chance to speak.

- Students can also make up their own statements of compassion to speak to one another.

"...A 'healing space' is where the bereaved child is given the opportunity to speak to others without any judgement, receiving validation for his or her many feelings and thoughts associtiated with grief. As a dialogue opens up, the child begins the process of leading *themself* through healing"...

from *The Evolution of Child Bereavement*
by Kids' Grief Relief

Session 2
All About Me

Objectives

* Students share how they're moving through the grieving process.

* Students create a timeline to review their lives from birth to present.

* Students share their personal story about the death of their loved one.

* Students compare how they feel inside versus how they show themselves to the outside world.

* Students share their greatest challenge.

* Students validate each other.

Materials Needed:
Two blank pieces of 8.5x11 paper for each student

Session 2
All About Me

Activities 7-11

Activity 7
How Am I Feeling Today?

Grief Support
Group

Poster #1

GRIEF

Poster #2

Procedure:

- Before the students arrive, place the initial two posters from the first session on the table.

- As the students come to group, ask them to write two words that describe their loved one next to the loved one's name on the poster.

- Students share what they have written.

- Next direct students to look at the poster list they created about GRIEF. Ask students to look at the words to describe what they are feeling through this next exercise.

- Give students a blank piece of paper, and ask them to use it to show how they are feeling. Students can crumple, tear, color, etc. the paper to express their grief.

- Ask students to share their creation with the group.

Activity 8
My Timeline

You've had many experiences throughout your life. Which ones do you always want to remember?

Write down at least five different memories that mean something to you.

Your timeline ends with the death of your loved one. You will have an opportunity to add to your timeline in another lesson.

MY TIMELINE

As you listen to others share their timeline, notice how different some of your memories are from the other students in your group. Also notice that some are the same as others.

©2014 Kids' Grief Relief   A-8

Procedure:

• Ask one student to read the top and bottom of Activity 8.

• Give each student a blank piece of paper, 8.5x11. Direct them to hold the paper long way (11" wide).

• Direct students to draw a horizontal 11" line in the middle of the paper, from one end to the other end (see diagram).

• On the left side of the 11"line, students draw a vertical line, and write their birthdate. On the middle of the 11" line, students draw a vertical line, and write the words "started school". On the right side of the 11" line, students draw a vertical line and write the date of the death of their loved one.

• Now the timeline is ready for students to fill in. Students may need guidance on writing down special events, suggest birthday parties, holidays, getting a special gift, going somewhere special with loved ones, first date, accomplishments, etc...

• Have the students save this paper in their folder for a future lesson.

Activity 9A-B
My Story

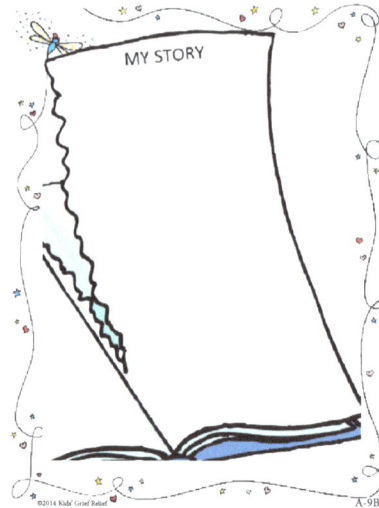

It's important to tell your story about the death of your loved one. What happened is part of your life forever. It's unique.

WRITE YOUR STORY ON THE NEXT PAGE USING THE PROMPTS BELOW

• Tell something about the relationship you had with your loved one before he/she died.

• What was your relationship like just before he/she died?"

• Tell about the day your loved one died. Where were you? How did you find out? Who was with you? Where did you go? How did you feel?

• Tell about the memorial service for your loved one. Was there a funeral? Did you participate? Was your loved one cremated? If so, where are the ashes?

• How did the rest of your family and friends react to the death?

• What was the worst part of the experience?

©2014 Kids' Grief Relief   A-9A

MY STORY

©2014 Kids' Grief Relief   A-9B

Procedure:

• Ask one student to read the top of Activity 9A.

• Read aloud each guideline as listed on Activity 9A.

• Turn to Activity 9B and give students time to write their story.

• When all students are done, ask them to share their stories.

• Remind students to practice Compassion as they listen "with their heart" to each other's stories.

Activity 10
Outside/Inside

Do other people in your life know how you are really feeling?

Does the outside you (what people see) match how you feel inside?

Sometimes when we grieve, we feel like we're wearing a mask. That's okay.

Outside Me   Inside Me

©2014 Kids' Grief Relief   A-10

Procedure:

- Ask one student to read the top of Activity 10.

- Tell students to draw and/or write words on the figures.

- Students may want to refer to the list of grief expressions that are listed on their poster.

- When completed, ask students to share.

- This can open a discussion on how we hide our feelings when we are grieving.

Activity 11
Validation of My
Greatest Challenge

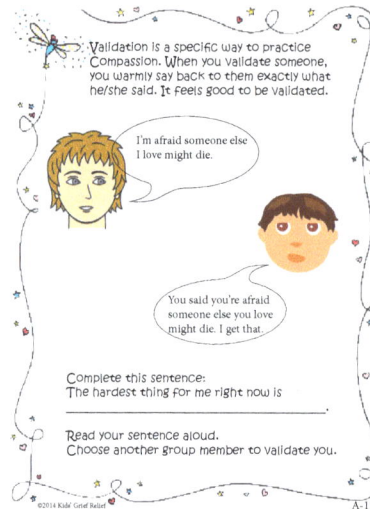

Validation is a specific way to practice Compassion. When you validate someone, you warmly say back to them exactly what he/she said. It feels good to be validated.

I'm afraid someone else I love might die.

You said you're afraid someone else you love might die. I get that.

Complete this sentence:
The hardest thing for me right now is

_____.

Read your sentence aloud.
Choose another group member to validate you.

©2014 Kids' Grief Relief   A-11

Procedure:

- Ask one student to read the top of Activity 11.

- Ask two different students to read the cartoon example of validation.

- Practice a few times by saying something and asking a student to validate you.

- Next direct students to complete the sentences on the bottom of Activity 11.

- When students have completed the sentence, direct them to validate each other as stated on the bottom of Activity 11.

"...Eventually, the grieving child is open to receive an understanding that all the thoughts and feelings of grief are a "normal" part of life. The child gives audience for a compassionate adult to support and lead him or her in finding their inner strength to heal. Understanding this lead role is a critical ingredient of the spiritual and emotional growth of the child"...

from *The Evolution of Child Bereavement*
by Kids' Grief Relief

Session 3
All About My Loved One

Objectives

✗ Students continue to assess how they're moving through the grieving process.

✗ Students share memories about their loved one.

✗ Students reflect about the death of their loved one.

✗ Students discuss where they believe their loved one's spirit has gone.

✗ Students continue to learn how to validate each other.

✗ Students envision the years ahead of them.

Materials Needed:

Game markers & One Die
Candy for Prizes
Blank piece of 8.5x11 paper for each student

Session 3
All About My Loved One

Activities 12-16

Mystie's Activities

12. How Am I Doing ?

13. Roll-A-Memory Game

14. Remembering

15. Reflections

16. My Future

Activity 12
How Am I Doing ?

Grief Support Group

Poster #1

GRIEF

Poster #2

Procedure:

- Before the students arrive, place the initial two posters from the first session on the table

- As the students come to group, ask them to write two words that describe themselves next to their name on the poster.

- Students share what they have written.

- Next direct students to look at the poster list they created about GRIEF. Ask students to write their initials next to the words that describe how they are feeling now.

- Ask each student to look at the poster with the initials, and choose another student to validate. For example, if a student put their initials next to the word "confused", another student can validate them by saying, "You feel confused today."

Activity 13
Roll-A-Memory Game

1	2	3	4	5
What is the first and last name of your special person?	Did your special person teach you anything?	Do you know your special person's birthday? (Day/Month/Year)	Was your special person buried or cremated?	Did your special person like to wear jewelery? What kind?
6 Describe a special holiday spent with your special person.	**7** Tell about the last time you saw your special person.	**8** What name did your special person call you?	**9** Tell about a funny moment with your special person.	**10** Describe a trip you took with your special person.
11 Tell about what kind of clothes your special person liked to wear.	**12** Tell about an object that reminds you of your special person.	**13** What kind of music did your special person enjoy?	**14** What kind of movies did your special person like to watch?	**15** Did your special person ever have a pet?
16 Did your special person have a favorite saying? What was it?	**17** Tell about a sad memory with your special person.	**18** Tell about some of the people who loved your special person.	**19** What one thing always makes you think about your special person?	**20** What's your favorite photo of your special person? Describe it.
21 Tell about something your special person loved to do.	**22** What time of day do you feel "dragged-down" over the death of your special person?	**23** What's the one thing you'll miss MOST about your special person?	**24** Do you feel peaceful about the way your special person was buried? Why?	**25** Tell about a gift you gave your special person.

©2014 Kids' Grief Relief   A-13

Procedure:

- Tell students that they will be playing a game for the purpose of sharing some memories about their loved one.

- Each student has his/her own board on Activity 12.

- Students choose a marker.

- Decide order of players.

- First person rolls the dice and moves that many spaces along his/her board.

- Student reads the question on the square. If student can answer the question, student circles the number on the square. If a student can't answer the question, direct him/her to put an X on the square, and skip that square and go to the next one he/she can answer.

- Next student follows the same procedure.

- Play a few rounds till each student has at least 8 numbers circled.

Activity 14
Remembering

What special things do you have to remind yourself about your special someone who died? Make a list.

1 ☆   4 ☆

2 ☆   5 ☆

3 ☆   6 ☆

Where do you keep your special things?

A-14

Procedure:

- Ask a student to read Activity 14 and give students time to complete the two activities.

- When completed, ask students to share.

Activity 15
Reflections

You're probably thinking a lot about your loved one.
Fill in the blanks below with some of your thoughts.

I wonder _____

I try _____

I understand _____

I want _____

I learned _____

I wish _____

I am _____

Where do you believe your special person's spirit is? Share your vision with the other students in your group, remembering that everyone has their own ideas about the afterlife.

©2014 Kids' Grief Relief   A-15

Procedure:

• Ask a student to read the top of Activity 15.

• When completed, ask students to share.

• At the bottom of Activity 15, students are invited to share where they believe their loved one's spirit has gone. This can open up a powerful discussion about beliefs in the afterlife. The most important consideration is that each student respects other's ideas, though the ideas may not be similar.

Activity 16
My Future

MY TIMELINE	FUTURE TIMELINE

MY TIMELINE

Birth   Started School   Death of Loved One

Age

FUTURE TIMELINE

Today   Six Months From Today   One Year From Today   Two Years From Today

Age

Procedure:

- This Activity can be done two ways:
    One piece of paper - front / back
    Two pieces of paper - side by side

- Direct students to find their Timelines from previous session. Instruct students to either use the blank side, or give them another 8.5 x 11 blank paper to create their Future Timeline.

- Direct students to create a Future Timeline, representing the next two years, by having them mark off today, six months, one year, and two years from the present date.

- Direct students to write down specific experiences they are planning in six months, one year, and in two years.

Activity 16
My Future

continued

Here's another opportunity to validate each other.

Listen to each other's plans for the next year, then choose one experience to validate. Add something positive after you validate your friend.

You can say something like, "that sounds like fun" or "good for you".

Next summer I'm going to be a junior counselor at my camp.

Next summer you're going to be a junior counselor at your camp. I bet you're going to have lots of fun.

©2014 Kids' Grief Relief   A-16

- When students have completed the Future Timeline, ask someone to read the top of Activity 16.

- Next ask two students to read the comic captions of the characters on Activity 16.

- One at a time, ask students to share what they have written on their Future Timeline, and ask another student to validate them.

Session 4
Self Reflections of Life/Death

Objectives

- Students continue to assess how they're moving through the grieving process.

- Students listen to the reading of *Diary of a Mystical Dragonfly*.

- Students gain a greater understanding of their own belief systems about life and death, through a self-assessment.

- Students gain an understanding of what things they can change/control and what things they can't change/control.

Materials Needed:

Diary of a Mystical Dragonfly

Session 4
Understanding Emotions

Activities 17-19

Mystie's Activities

17. Am I Feeling Different ?

18.1-18.7   Reading/Reflecting from
Diary of a Mystical Dragonfly

19. Can / Can't Change

Activity 17
What's Changing ?

Grief Support
Group

Poster #1

GRIEF

Poster #2

Procedure:

- Before the students arrive, place Poster #1 and Poster#2 on the table.

- As the students come to group, ask them to look at the poster created about GRIEF. Ask them to find their initials from the week before.

- If they feel the same as last week, they can circle their initials. If they do not feel the same, they can put an X on their initials. If they feel something different this week, ask them to write their initials next to the words that describe their feelings.

- Students share what they have written.

- Direct students to Poster#1. Ask them to draw a heart around their name and the name of their loved one, using a color that represents the relationship they shared.

- Students share why they chose their specific color.

Activity 18-1 to 18-7
Diary of A Mystical Dragonfly

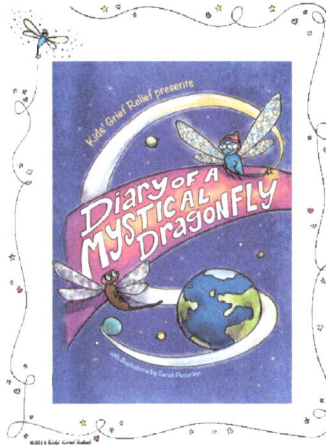

Procedure:

- Show students soft bound copy of <u>Diary of A Mystical Dragonfly</u>. Tell them <u>you</u> will be summarizing the book for them, one chapter at a time. Each chapter is summarized on pages 42-46.

- Alternately, if time is available, you may read the book to them one chapter at a time.

- Direct students to A-18 in Mystie's Activites, which shows the cover of the book.

- Tell the students the story is about life and death. The main character of the story is a dragonfly from another planet, who enthusiastically travels to earth, only to be devistated by the death of a new found friend.

Activity 18-1 to 18-7
Diary of A Mystical Dragonfly

continued

- There are seven chapters in the book. The students have a title page and picture for each chapter. (pgs.18-1to 18-7) Under each picture are written statements.

- After a chapter is summarized orread aloud, invite the students to silently read each statement from the cooresponding chapter, in Mystie's Activities. Students are instructed to use a 1 to 5 scale, 5 meaning they completely agree with the statement, and 1 meaning they completely disagree.

- <u>After</u> all students have completed their rating from a chapter, invite students to share their numbers.

Activity 18-1 to 18-7
Diary of A Mystical Dragonfly

continued

- For example, from the first statement of 18-1:

1. I like my name. _____
(1-5)

- One at a time, students read the statement aloud, along with their number rating. After all the students have shared, invite them to expand the idea, if they so choose. Remind students that there is no right or wrong rating. The purpose of the ratings are for students' reflections, possibly with the idea that in the future, the rating may or may not change.

- Some statements are open-ended for students to expand on, if they choose. For example, from 18-7:

5. I know what my greatest strength is. _____
(1-5)

- Invite students to acturally share what they believe their greatest strength is.

Activity 18-1 to 18-7
Diary of A Mystical Dragonfly

Chapter 1 & 2 Summary

Chapter 1

- Mystie - or Mystic A. Dragonfly - is a mystical, magical dragonfly from the planet Nilrem. The planet Nilrem is one of Peace, Harmony, and Love.

- Mystie is a Mystic - meaning she is connected to her own inner spirit. She is also magical - meaning she uses her inner magical power to fly around Nilrem.

Chapter 2

- Growing up, Mystie started without wings. While focusing on her thoughts and feelings of Love, she found her wings started to grow.

- Mystie learned pracitce makes perfect when it came to flying. She kept flying, and had fewer and fewer crashes as she kept focused. Soon she mastered flying like a Dragonfly.

Activity 18-1 to 18-7
Diary of A Mystical Dragonfly

Chapter 3 & 4 Summary

Chapter 3

- Mystie announced she was going to Earth. Her grandpa said,"That's not the best place for you"... "It's hard to use your magic there..." "The last dragonfly came back with some shocking and unsettling information.."

- That just made it more interesting for Mystie - she HAD to find out what made Earth so special ! After a going-away party, Mystie flew toward Earth.

- Mystie settled in the Lowcountry - where she saw birds, animals, the marsh, the ocean, and met Lark - a dolphin.

Chapter 4

- One day Mystie met Darvy - an Earth Dragonfly. They became best friends, and eventually fell in love. Mystie's magic worked magnificiently here on Earth !

- After six weeks together, Darvy fell to the ground; dead. Mystie was hysterical - on Nilrem dragonflies live forever - and death doesn't exist. Mystie yelled for help.

- Lark expained that Darvy's death was normal for Earth dragonflies, who live a short life, but live each day to the fullest. "What kind of place is this, anyway ?" Mystie said crying.

Activity 18-1 to 18-7
Diary of A Mystical Dragonfly

Chapter 5 & 6 Summary

Chapter 5

- Darvy's friends of all kinds came to his funeral. All of them spoke of how they missed him, and had fun with him. Mystie spoke, but couldn't finish her words.

- They buried Darvy. Lark told Mystie, "His spirit is alive in a place called Heaven, where he will be forever happy and peaceful.

Chapter 6

- Mystie couldn't fly anymore - her wings felt heavy and dragged on the ground. She had lots of feelings and judgements abouyt Darvy's death - anger, unfairness, crying, confusion...

- Mystie wanted to go home but she was a mess ! Her magic was gone.

- Lark explained that Mystie was grieving because she loved Darvy. As Lark talked about Love, Mystie's wings became a bit stronger.

- Ultimately, Mystie switched her thoughts and feelings from Grief (Dragged Down) to the Love she had for Darvy. She didn't have to see Darvy to know she loved him. Eventually, she got her flying back.

Activity 18-1 to 18-7
Diary of A Mystical Dragonfly

Chapter 7 Summary

Chapter 7

- It was time for Mystie to end her Earth adventure and go home. The last of her friends to say good-bye to was Lark.

- Lark said it was tough for Earthlings to move through grief. She asked Mystie to stay and help Earthlings to move through grief the same way she did.

- Lark also said that Mystie could remind Earthlings that they can use their inner powers to move through grief.

- Lark then asked Mystie to think about staying to help. After one week, Mystie said "YES", - and prepared herself for her first mission.

Activity 19
Can/Can't Change

- List what things in life I can control/change:

- List what things in life I can't control/change:

Procedure:

- This Activity asks students two thought-provoking questions. Give them time to write their answers.

- For the group discussion, do one question at a time.

- This Activity is also an opportunity for students to practice Validating each other.

"...As a child processes the difficult thoughts and emotions associated with grief, love all-ways triumphs. Our society is greatly blessed by compassionate children who grow up loving themselves and others"...

from *The Evolution of Child Bereavement*
by Kids' Grief Relief

Session 5
Change Your Thoughts
Change Your Experience

Objectives

✳ Students become aware that their thoughts have a direct effect on their experience.

✳ Students uncover their own negative thinking patterns that do not serve them.

✳ Students release negative thoughts in a kinesthetic exercise.

✳ Students create new, powerful affirmations.

✳ Students gain a greater sense of their inner strengths to move through grief.

Materials Needed:

Waste Basket
Scrap Paper
Hand Mirror

Session 5
Change Your Thoughts
Change Your Experience
Activities 20-23

Mystie's Activities

20. Checking In

21. What You Think Matters

22A-B. Affirmations

23. Frame Yourself!

Activity 21
Checking In

Procedure:

- Before the students arrive, place Poster #1 and Poster#2 on the table.

- Direct students to Poster #1. Ask them to draw some sort of symbol (like a tatoo) that represents how they feel about their loved one.

- As the students come to group, ask them to look at Poster #2. Ask students if any of the listed thoughts/ feelings about grief moved through them during the last week. If so, direct them to write their initials by the words, along with the date.

Activity 22
What You Think Matters

WHAT YOU THINK MATTERS

Guess how many thoughts most people think in one day? Over 12,000!

Positive thoughts create positive experiences.

Yet, when you're grieving, you probably have a lot of dragged-down thoughts. That's normal.

Any of these feel familiar?

It's terrible that I'll never see _____ again.

I wish I could change what happened.

My life is all messed up now.

I keep thinking about how _____ died.

If only I could have _____ maybe _____ wouldn't have died.

It's not fair!

What if someone else dies?

I should have been nicer to _____.

©2014 Kids' Grief Relief   A-22

Procedure:

- Ask one student to read the top of Activity 22.

- Ask one student at a time to read the sentences on the page. Ask students if what they read feels familiar to them, thus opening a discussion of the thoughts they're experiencing while they're in the grieiving process.

- Next give each student a blank piece of paper, 8.5x11. Have them fold it in half three times to make eight different sections.

- Ask them to write down each "trash" thought on a different section of the paper. They then tear the paper on the crease so they have separate thoughts on each piece of paper.

- Place a trash basket near the students. One at time, ask the student to read one trash thought aloud. Some students will not want to share.

- Next direct the student to rip-up the piece of paper and put it in the trash.

- Do this until they all have thrown away their written thoughts.

Activities 23A-B
Affirmations

Now that you've thrown away your "trash thoughts", it's time to replace them with powerful, affirming thoughts. An affirming thought declares a truth.

Your true nature is Love. Love is more than an emotion because it's energy is always present inside you. Love IS you!

The love you feel for your loved one is forever. The energies of grief will move through you, but Love remains. That's Powerful!

Affirming thoughts come from Love, which means they come from the truth of who you are. Take a look at the thoughts on the next page.

Can you feel the POWER in those thoughts?

©2014 Kids' Grief Relief   A-23A

1. I am brave.
2. I am smart enough to understand what happened.
3. It feels good to talk to others about what happened.
4. I have my own unique feelings about death.
5. I have special memories of _____ that I will always treasure.
6. I like who I am.
7. I am grateful for all the people who love me.
8. I am a powerful kid!
9. I can find healthy ways to let go of anger.
10. I am capable to handle what's going on in in my life.
11. I choose relationships with people who appreciate me for who I am.

©2014 Kids' Grief Relief   A-23B

Procedure:

- Ask one student to read the top of Activity 23A, and another student to read the bottom.

- Direct students to silently read the listed affirmations on Activity 23 B.

- Next ask each student to speak aloud their two favorite affirmations from the list.

- Tell students that whenever they catch themselves thinking a "trash thought" they can replace it with an affirming thought.

- Tell students that for affirmations to really help them with their grief, it's important for them to repeat the words to themselves.

Activity 24
Frame Yourself!

Procedure:

- Direct students to Activity 24.

- Direct students to draw a picture of themselves inside the frame.

- On the outside of the frame, students write down four positive affirmations about themselves. They may write on each side of the four sides of the frame.

- Using a hand-mirror, invite each student to look in the mirror, then speak aloud the four affirmations around their picture.

- As a Validation activity, ask students to validate each other with at least one affirmation that was shared.

NOTE:
Tell students they have one session left, and remind them to bring in a picture of their deceased loved one for the ending celebration.

Session 6
<u>Release and Celebrate !</u>

Objectives

- Students share what they have learned about grief.

- Students create a ceremony to honor their loved one.

- Students experience some closure in their relationship with their loved one.

- Students share in a celebration as an ending of their experience in the group.

<u>Materials Needed:</u>

Battery operated tea-lights for each student
Scissors
Food and Drink for each student
Optional Graduation Gift for each student

(e.g. available from Kids' Grief Relief - see pg.4)

Session 6
Release and Celebrate !

Activities 24-29

Mystie's Activities

24. Last Look at Posters

25. Letters of Love

**26. Special Ceremony
to Honor Our Loved Ones**

27. Forever Calendar

28. Celebrate !

29. ... And now ...

Activity 24
Last Look at Posters

Grief Support Group Poster #1	GRIEF Poster #2

Procedure:

- Before the students arrive, place the initial two posters from the first session on the table

- Direct students to the Poster #2. Invite students to write down anything else about their loved one they would like to share.

- Tell students they can cut out and take home their piece of the poster at the end of the session.

- Direct students to the Poster #1, defining GRIEF. Ask, *"If you had a friend who experienced the death of a loved one, what would you tell them about Grief? What advice would you give?"* Allow time for students to share their ideas.

  This is a good way for you to assess what each student has learned about grief.

Activity 25
Letters of Love

Procedure:

- Direct students to write a letter **TO** their deceased loved one. Tell students they can *choose* to share the letter at the ending celebration during this final session.

Note:

Some students may need some writing prompts. You may want to write them down where all the students can see them.
Here are some suggestions:

> "I always wanted to tell you..."
> "I wish you could have..."
> "What I really miss is..."
> "I'm feeling...."
> "When I think about you I..."

- After the letter is finished, ask students to pretend to be their special person and write a letter **FROM** their special person to themselves. Again, they may choose to share the letter during the ending celebration.

Activity 26
Special Ceremony
to Honor Our Loved Ones

Procedure:

- Give each student a battery operated candle. (provided)

- Direct them to write the name of their loved one on the plastic side. (Sharpies work best)

- Create an empty space on a table, where the students can place their candles in a circle. Students can place photos of their loved one next to their candle. You may want to use the poster of their loved one's names, as the centerpiece. If you choose to do this, direct students to place their battery operated candle near their piece on the poster.

- One at a time, ask the students to turn their candle on. Remind them that the light of the candle represents the love and light in their hearts, which will be present for their loved for the rest of their lives.

- As the students light their candles, they may read one or both letters.

Activity 27
Forever Calendar

FOREVER CALENDAR

During each and every day,
We Love them.

During each and every night,
We Love them.

During each and every week,
We Love them.

During each and every month,
We Love them.

During each and every season,
We Love them.

During each and every year,
We Love them.

As the days turn into weeks, turn into months,
turn into seasons, turn into years,
We Love them;
Forever.

©2016 Kids' Grief Relief · A-28

Procedure:

- When all candles are lit, and each student has had the opportunity to read their letters, read aloud together the *Forever Calendar* on Activity 28.

- Ask students if there is anything else they would like to say before their candle is turned off.

- As the students turn off their candle, reminding them to keep the candle as a special remembrance of their loved one.

Activity 28
Celebrate !

Grief Support Group

Poster #1

Procedure:

- Tell students that in honor of their loved ones, and in honoring their commitment to move through grief, there will be a celebration with food and drink.

- During the celebration, direct students to cut apart their piece of the Grief Support Group poster with their name and their loved one's name, and take it home.

- Tell students to read the last page in *Mystie's Activities*. They are invited to receive a free e-book from Mystie!

- Hand out "Graduation Gift" (optional).

- ENJOY!

Note
Kids' Grief Relief offers special mementos for students who have completed this course (e.g. Mystie Bracelet or Keychain).

Activity 29
... And now ...

I used Diary writing to help me move through my grief.

What will you continue to do?

Procedure:

- Tell students to read the last page in *Mystie's Activities*. With the group, brainstorm ways each student can/will continue to move through grief, now that the group sessions have ended.

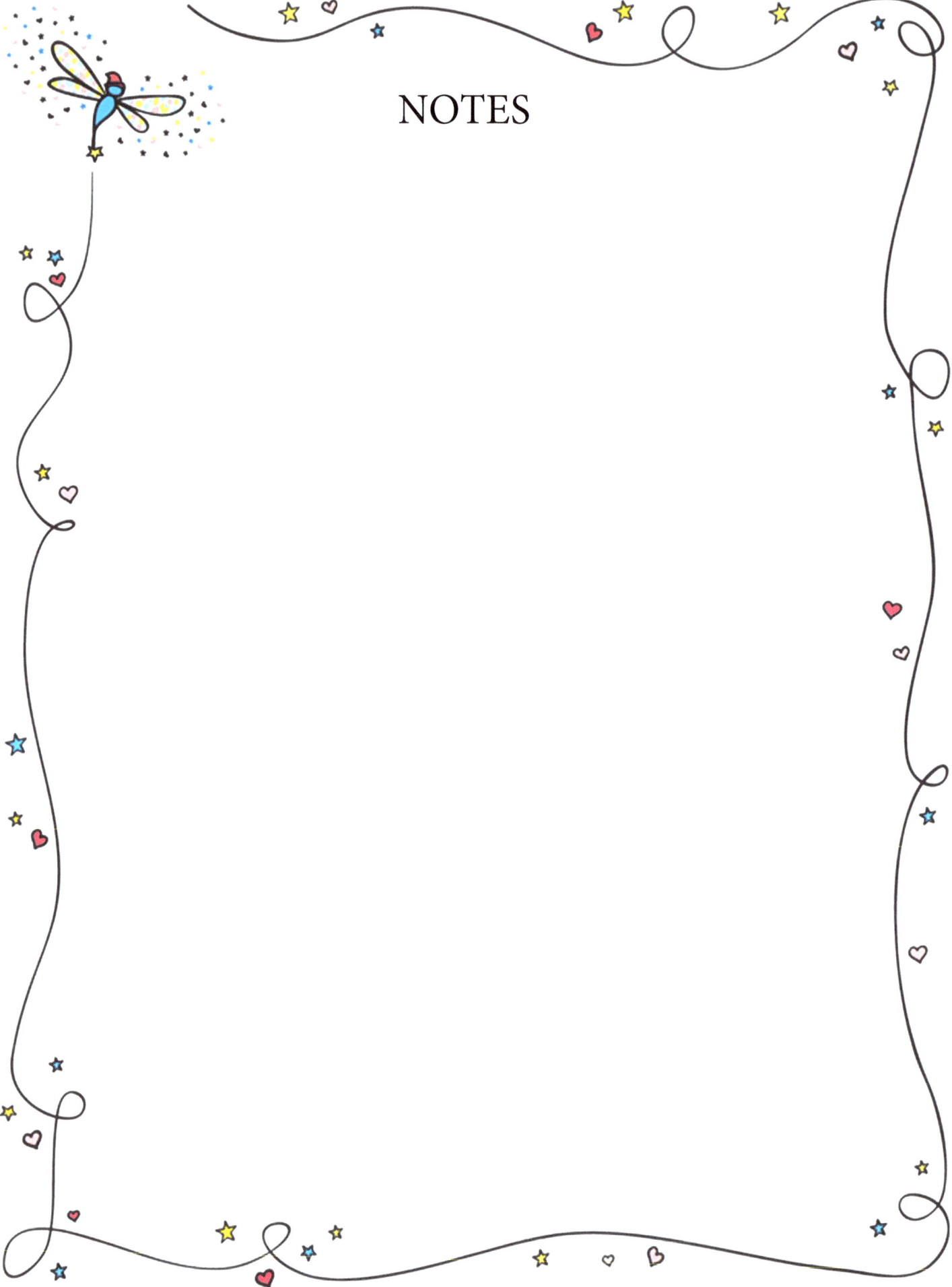

NOTES